With God All Things Are Possible!

Copyright 2016

All rights reserved

ISBN 9780998307879
ISBN 0998307874

All rights reserved. No part of this publication may be reproduced in any means, in any way, without the permission, in writing, from the Copyright owner. A product of Skookum Books
864 552 1055

Dedication: To my husband Dean, a most faithful, most loving, generous man. We hardly know what life is like without each other. Growing up together, and growing together, we weathered through many conflicts, and had wonderful experiences in our lifetime. We played tennis for over sixty years and made a mighty, good team. We enjoyed all the great experiences provided us by our three sons. They are intelligent, witty men, who have given us many reasons to be proud! They have been very loving, generous, thoughtful, and righteous men!

Acknowledgement: My life has been identified by my years of teaching my fourth graders. They made me a better person and I thank each and everyone of them!

Skookum Book's Charms

The beautiful butterfly, that graces our flowers and bushes, goes through a mysterious and magical change in becoming an adult! The Greeks believed each time a butterfly emerges from it's cocoon, a new human soul is born! Legend has it that whispering a wish to a butterfly, then releasing it to carry the wish to heaven, will make the wish come true! Perhaps this is when they acquire little clouds on their wings! The butterfly is a symbol of fresh life, happiness, and joy! The "night butterfly", the moth, is attracted to a flame and light, just like our souls are attracted to heavenly truths!

Hummingbirds are active, beautiful additions to our gardens, who give us a sense of life, nature's beauty, and fresh life! These "flying jewels" flit from flower to flower picking up and delivering pollen so that life can continue! It's the creature that opens the heart and shows the truth of beauty! It brings laughter and enjoyment and the magic of being alive! The hummingbird stands for spreading love and joy!

God and Country, Two Sets of Laws for Teens!

Betty Lou Rogers

Illustrated by
Jenison Hardin

Laws are the rules that are needed,
For people to live together in peace,
Since some people choose to act wrongly,
Someone must make bad behavior cease!

For everyone to live undisturbed,
There are two sets of rules we should follow,
1. The Bible tells how to act and behave,
2. Our country's rules give the order we crave!

If every person had friendly intentions,
And cared for the welfare of others,
We wouldn't need to have laws and rules,
We wouldn't need lawmen controlling the fools!

If every person respected life,
And valued the worth of their neighbors,
Officers of the law would not get killed,
Protecting us from all the ill-willed!

If every person was welfare-minded,
For friends and strangers alike,
Wars would not happen, we'd have only peace,
Happiness would reign, sorrow would cease!

If goodwill guided the people in our world,
We wouldn't find fault and complain,
No one would suffer from hunger and thirst,
We wouldn't have to fear, those acting their worst!

If everyone behaved with virtue in mind,
Every thought, word, or act was for good,
We'd never have killings and murders,
For safety, not look any further!

If we all were so proud of our nation,
And aware of the treasures it holds,
We'd be thankful for the privileges offered,
And guard them with brashness, that's bold!

If we all were so proud of our nation,
We wouldn't be burning our flag,
Our flag stands for the independence and values,
That allows people to act up and nag!

Now, we all are so proud of our country,
We're aware of those things needing change,
We need to work hard to correct things,
Instead of destroying and acting deranged!

If we obeyed the rules of the heart,
And abide by the laws of our land,
If our leaders are doing the job they should do,
We'll be safe and secure, filled with gratitude!

God decrees we obey our country's rules,
We should honor our homeland this way.
Our nation is strong with fair and just laws,
United we are, with liberty and justice for all!

We are citizens of two worlds,
And each have their own special rules,
We learn God's rules from the Bible,
We learn our country's rules at school!

God gave us rules that number ten,
Their purpose is to keep us safe,
They give directions for how to live,
They grant us the freedom that only God gives!

God's rules are about morality and love,
Which leads toward happiness,
Our country's rules help keep the peace,
So we live with order and harmony!

God is a very loving God,
He want's what is right for us all,
He wants us to be happy, safe, and secure,
He wants our lives to be wholesome and pure!

Our heavenly kingdom touts the law of love,
Love does no harm to its neighbors
Love cares and provides for people's needs,
Love overcomes evil, out-laws misdeeds!

God gave us laws to show how special we are,
Those who are wise will rejoice for this care,
Those who rebel and object to the rules,
Won't get very far, for rebellion's not cool!

Following and obeying laws made by man,
Will help us feel calm and composed,
It also will make our country strong and sure,
Having an honest nation, makes us secure!

Following the laws that our country holds dear,
Leads to a contented, and happier life,
Laws warn us of danger, protect us from harm,
They free us from guilt, but set off alarms!

This journey we're on, has choices to make,
It's wise to have a good map to guide,
You'll find many hazards along the way,
With the right guidance, you'll not go astray!

We are Pilgrims, traveling through this life,
We have the rules and guidelines to follow,
We can seek and find the support we need,
So, each day we grow, we're sure to succeed!

With wicked people in charge, sin will grow,
Every group's attitude comes from the top,
Followers will act just like those who lead,
Making it easier to commit misdeeds!

The laws of our land are written down to see,
It's easy to understand what they mean,
And if you believe, and make a good start,
You'll find God's laws, are written on your heart!

God's law says, "Instead of harming others,
Do good to them, as you'd like done to you,"
This is the kindness to give every day,
It's the love and mercy we all should convey!

Whoever is dishonest with little,
Will also be dishonest with much,
God calls us to be honest people,
To be devoted, and filled with trust!

We won't be condemned for what we don't know,
What we do know, we should do with force,
Knowing what's right, and doing what's wrong,
Is putting the cart, before the horse!

Smart, wise people know their limits,
They know what they are able to do,
They won't hide, what they do not know,
They won't dodge, they'll be open and true!

When we hear of trouble and stress,
We know who first will be called,
The police are ready to save and protect,
We should honor them, with our respect!

Police are the ones who's lives are cut short,
They meet wickedness, in their work, everyday,
Trouble and problems pop up like a storm,
Yet, ever and always, the police lead the way!

One thing's for sure, when the chips are down,
Police officers are one of a kind,
They'll give up their lives, while protecting yours,
They watch over us all, fighting evil and crime!

The police bring order, to a disordered world,
They generate safety, out of hostile conditions,
They produce peace, where there's ugly unrest,
They have compassion for the hurt and unblessed!

Those who keep you on the straight and narrow,
Are your teachers, and the officers in blue,
Your teachers are your parents at school,
The police are the angels who save you from fools!

If your dad was an officer of the law,
There would likely be exciting stories to hear,
But you'd never be sure he'd always come home,
'Cause he's in danger, fighting evil, wherever it roams!

These guardians, our knights in shining armor,
Make sure our lives are safe as they can be,
Their selfless devotion to protect and defend,
We should appreciate them and also commend!

If we worry about what we cannot do,
We won't concentrate on what we can,
We'll miss, all the times, we can assist and protect,
We might even miss saving some from neglect!

If you have sinned and broken a law,
The second time, it's much easier to do,
Doing what's wrong, might fill you with gloom,
While doing good deeds, improves attitudes!

A city on a hill cannot be hidden away,
Because of the bright lights it sends out,
Good people have those same beams of light,
Transform the darkness, with your own rays, so bright!

If you are aware of God's main theme,
And you've not been friendly and kind,
You must revise and revamp what you've done,
Have some, do good, feel good, love good fun!

God gave you to your parents,
You belong to them, but only for awhile,
Follow their rules and hold them dear.
Love and honor them and keep them near!

God also says to never steal,
Don't take what belongs to another,
You have no right to cause other's pain,
To your mother, you'll find it hard to explain!

Friendliness produces joy and pleasure,
When you aid and help someone, too,
If you've guided someone out of distress,
You've been an angel wiping away tears, no less!

Have you ever looked around your world,
At the beauty of flowers and trees,
The blue of water and the sky,
And love your land, home of the free!

If you will take a really good look,
And see all that's decent in your life,
You have to know from where this comes,
It's part of God's plan, it's communion!

You should remember, in the still of the night,
To be thankful and express gratitude,
God's goodness and love are there by your side,
To guide and forgive, to comfort and decide!

If you think about the wonder of life,
And the battle between evil and good,
Choosing God's goodness, makes hearts really soar,
Being helpful and kind, spreads good feelings galore!

God's home is a beautiful, wonderful place,
No sadness, nor tears, only delight,
You probably would like to end up there,
But those who kill and maim, go elsewhere!

We are one nation under God,
This fact. all who come here, should know,
If newcomers do not like this fact,
They should go somewhere else, to be exact!

We can lead healthy and wholesome lives,
By honoring our country and God,
We obey our laws of church and state,
We are peaceful and righteous at any rate!

We've been given a wonderful place,
To live, and love, play, and grow,
To laugh and cry, to sing and rejoice,
For a God who loves, forgives, and knows!

Faith, hope, love, and joy,
What more could anyone want?
No more tumult, turmoil, and tears,
Full of thankfulness, free of fear!

Now, if you should grow weary, and full of doubt,
You want to be someone worth noting,
So, what do you do, when you feel so defeated?
"Treat others the way you'd like to be treated!"

And always remember, never forget - - - -

America is your homeland,
'Twas won with blood and strife,
And cherish all our freedoms,
And guard them with your life!

This is your book! You can be a champion of Law and Order.

1. Find a police man or woman in your neighborhood or area.

2. What is their name? _____

3. What is their favorite sport? _____

4. What is their scariest experience? _____
_____

5. What is their funniest experience? _____
_____

6. What is their favorite food?_____

7. Can you find something good to do for this person, that would show your appreciation for their courage and bravery in caring for everyone?

8. What did you do?_____
_____

About the Author

Betty Lou Rogers is a retired fourth grade teacher from Madison Elementary School in Sandusky, Ohio. Her strategy for success was simple. Engage! Work together! Be active learners! Then employ her "one more chance" philosophy!

Betty Lou Rogers grew up in rural northwestern Ohio, graduating from Fremont Ross High School. She married her childhood sweetheart and raised three sons. During this time, she returned to college where she graduated with a B. S. Degree in Elementary Education from Bowling Green State University, in Bowling Green, Ohio. She was a member of the prestigious educational society, Kappa Delta Pi.

While teaching at Madison School, Mrs. Rogers was keenly aware of what children needed, both as a group and as individuals, in effectual learning in the classroom. She also had the intuition to know how to accomplish this by challenging her students to be active learners, as opposed to the sit, listen, and absorb approach! Always have lesson material in front of the student, so they are actively participating in the lesson, never pushing the child beyond their ability, but always working toward the best they can do! Often times the student is awakened to and surprised by their own ability. Mrs. Rogers' most telling educational approach was offering the children "one more chance" to learn and succeed, by giving open-book tests!

Tests show what the student hasn't learned! "My job is to give the children every opportunity to learn." This strategy caused her students to become more familiar with the contents and location of information in their books. This offering, enabled them to find the answer, complete the test, and learn what was missed before. These answers could even be more meaningful to them! When parents found this out, there was no excuse for a failing grade!

Mrs. Rogers was also a Jennings Scholar, which honored and rewarded teachers in the elementary classroom. The Jennings Foundation provides a means for greater accomplishment, on the part of teachers, with the hope it would result in greater recognition for those in the teaching profession within the public school system.

Mrs. Rogers is a member of Advent United Methodist Church in Simpsonville, S.C. Besides writing, she loves her sewing and crafts, and gardening! Mrs. Rogers and her husband have four granddaughters, and seven great-grandchildren!

After twenty-seven years of teaching, Mrs. Rogers philosophy for success has permeated the American landscape through her students in both academic and professional fields. Her love for teaching and writing, can never be equaled in any way, except her hope for students to find her writing truly illuminating!

Mrs. Rogers' previously published works:

The Thimseagle Thievers
Change Can Be Good!
Paste and Gluey, A Sticky Tale!

New publications coming:

Kate Earns Her MBA in Manners, Behavior, Attitude!
Chris Earns His MBA in Manners, Behavior, Attitude!
A new series of books for preteens and teens:
It's So Important To Be Honest!
The Ten Commandments for Teens, and Helpful Hints In-Between!
Proverbs, The First Book Written For the Young, Plus A Little Bit For Everyone!
Acquiring the Human Skills of Thinking, Saying, and Doing, for Teens!
A Medley of Options for the "Not Yet Old" Set!
God and Country. Two Sets of Laws for Teens!
The Human Dilemma of the Young, The Scramble for PAM! Power, Approval, and Money, (Ecclesiastes)
A Hodge-Podge of Thoughts for Teens, That's Not Gibberish!
Law and Order for Teens: Ignore or Restore!
ABC's For Teens, and What They Mean!
So, You Think We Shouldn't Have Dropped "The Bomb"?
For fun: Bossy Susie Saucy and Capricious Caleb O'Connor

God and Country, Two Sets of Laws for Teens! This book, written in verse, explores why we need rules and laws. It breaks the laws into two parts, God's rules and our country's rules. Both are necessary and acceptable. Our safety depends on the rule of law! God supports our country's laws!

Other published works by Betty Lou Rogers:

Proverbs, The First Book Written for the Young!
The Ten Commandments for Teens, and Helpful Hints In-Between
It's So Important To Be Honest!
The Thimseagle Thievers
Change Can Be Good!
Paste and Gluey, A Sticky Tale!

Mrs. Rogers books are published under:
Skookum Books.com

www.ingramcontent.com/pod-product-compliance
Lightning Source LLC
Chambersburg PA
CBHW041231040426
42444CB00002B/125